SPLICE

Splice

by Anthony Borruso

Copyright © July 1, 2025 by Anthony Borruso

No part of this book may be used or performed without written consent of the author, if living, except for critical articles or reviews.

Borruso, Anthony
1st edition

ISBN: 978-1-949487-34-3
Library of Congress Control Number: 2024939547

Interior design by Hadley Hendrix
Cover design by Joel W. Coggins
Primary Editing by Natasha Kane
Supporting Editing by Patrick Werle

Trio House Press, Inc.
Minneapolis
www.triohousepress.org

"What is it that characterizes montage,
and consequently, its embryo the shot?
Collision. A conflict between two adjoining pieces.
Conflict. Collision."

–Sergei Eisenstein

"Don't laugh at the fear
of the man next to me, leaping from his seat,
but ask yourself, how long you could focus
your eye on your own approaching destruction."

–A. Van Jordan

"Its existence
Was real, though troubled, and the ache
Of this waking dream can never drown out
The diagram still sketched on the wind,
Chosen, meant for me and materialized
In the disguising radiance of my room."
–John Ashbery

Table of Contents

Atmospheric Skull Sodomizing a Grand Piano   13

I

In Defense of Voice-over   17

A Hypochondriac Walks into Fourteen Lines   18

Fast-Fish and Loose-Fish   19

Watching Jeopardy I Start to Feel Sad   20

Under the Water or Whistling   21

Steve Buscemi   22

On Symbiosis   23

Foramen Magnum   24

The Most Beautiful Suicide   26

Semi-Autobiography as SNL Cast Member   28

In Preparation of Storms   29

II

Like Bartleby's   33

Resonance Imaging   34

Thelonius Monk   36

Emerson Synecdoche   37

At the Reception Desk   38

Tabula Rasa	39
5G Golden Shovel	41
Ballad of Ted Williams	43
Proposition	44

III

Void-Song	49
Self-Portrait With an Open Skull	50
Frances McDormand	51
Thoreau in Williamsburg	52
Scorsese Dreamsong	53
Ode to R. Budd Dwyer	55
Yorick,	56
Decasia: The State of Decay	58
Bill Murray	59
Another Dusky Sonnet	60
Digging My Own Grave	61
Man on Bus #2	62
After Surgery, My Father Helps Me Bathe	63

IV

The Rogue Patient	67
Murphy's Law	68

The Sunday Scaries	70
Tilda Swinton	71
A Vindication	72
Love-Sloshed Cinema	73
Hook's Soliloquy	74
When You Come Around Everything Else Disappears	75
Sirens' Lexicon	76

Post-credits Scene

Chuang-Tzu Golden Shovel	81
Notes	83
Acknowledgements	85
About the Author	89

Atmospheric Skull Sodomizing a Grand Piano

after Salvador Dalí

It is a gross thing to see sound submit
itself to skull; with ivory insistence
the slack jaw lifts the cherry lid—music
abounds, but is no less deformed

than forms found in a downsloping desert:
eye socket slouched in ecstasy,
canoe skulking toward golden nowhere.
Still life with unseen malady. Do you hear

Lorca, miles deep in mirage, pleading
take me poetic jolt, eccentric sky, man-
handle me with the selfsame beak
that broke Leda. For love is honed in

onanism and hopelessness. The pianist
cracks his fingers with anticipation
then pounds a ruinous instrument.
This is the world we live in; you can look

away or stroke an *I* like a shadow
fondling its lack, but behind that
sunbaked abode you sculpted
objects turn pliant, unreasonable, swollen

with honest deception, they roll
in the throes of an ossified song.

I

In Defense of Voice-over

after Charlie Kaufman

Do I have an original thought in my head   Does anyone
What about an epiphyte   Does it bloom with the same
knowledge that's stored in a tree's trunk   How Darwinian
to worry yourself weary, to project your existence
off an anonymous gnarled back   It's Valentine's day
I'm surrounded by packing bubbles   postcards   Ellipses
plink from my stopped sink   Technically the procedure
is brain damage   Malkovich is a vessel   And I only have
to use the source material loosely   My head is a vessel
This train throbbing to Montauk is a vessel   My love
too and the sunny months we spent quoting romcoms
Vessels   What if in sleep someone   picks the lock
of my eardrum   What if I'm not the protagonist
What if I wrote a poem as Charlie while Charlie
was writing a poem as me   Is this natural
selection   Are viruses alive or do they merely hijack
the living   John Cusack thieving consciousness
in the glint of someone else's eyes   Am I a virus
or a minimalist drawing   of a person scrutinizing his creator
Damning his use of voice-over   caesura   artifice
and how sometimes they reach across the lacuna to
catch something almost real   A satchel full
of fetishes   phobias   the hope of ending things
or at least feeling   for a moment like the octopus
with his three hearts and eight limbs   overwhelmingly

A Hypochondriac Walks into Fourteen Lines

Poundcake, earthquake, paranoiac zest, I
feel the flaw within my chest, the moon is
crumbling at its crest—Jesus Christ
I'm a masochist, coughing river-brack
and wood chips, the headache and thought itch of
terminating consciousness. What's the over-
under on my being being six feet lower?
Why's this salamander got his tail wrapped
round my tumors? Terminus to terminus,
Tallahassee to Kalamazoo, my body's
that Banksy that shreds itself; it hums a
Morricone soundtrack facing off against the mind:
aneurysm, melanoma, heart attack,
on a toothpick I sample each savory demise.

Fast-Fish and Loose-Fish

As if he could grab Texas by the panhandle, man thinks whatever
he jabs is his. Lob a harpoon into a blubbery back, and it's
fit to hitch beside the bulwark. Thrust a flag into a craterous
plunder, and the tide rises and falls at his command. Is not possession
the hole of the law? Don't the commons make you weep? Wistful sailor, droll
cowboy, frontiers of ambiguous blue and brown wait to be plated
on maps. A bandit carries hate across the Sonoran desert, sips
it judiciously from a leather flask. What belongs to anyone
seems increasingly slippery, take the lines crammed into this sonnet
and the meanings that heave inside each word, take the dreadful bone-white whale
I've managed to stick with a waif-pole after three days of hard chase; they
are mine, for now. But soon, according to unwritten rule, I too will
slip into death's dirt and democratization, abandoning flesh
to reclaim my ribcage and plagiarize the poetics of earthworms.

Watching Jeopardy I Start to Feel Sad

Not cornflower melancholy, but snowdrift
wistful. The sadness one feels as the last block
of Irish cheddar departs the charcuterie board.

It's quizzical. How the contestants just stand there
as forest fires flame and children suck nicotine
steam from flash drives. As Alexa distills

metadata from our domestic spats. Comical
too. *What is a Stradivarius? What are varicose
veins?* Every answer eliciting a question—

every question thrashing on the carpet
like a flea-ridden rottweiler. What was that
Monty Python sketch? The one with the dead

parrot and the shopkeep who refuses
to acknowledge its deceased state? That's what
this is like, mouthing answers, feckless, Trebek

and I, holding each other hostage,
perfecting the art of feigning knowledge.

Under the Water or Whistling

after John Berryman

Unfortunately, no one believes I'm insane
as I say—I climb bridges, I wade
into merciless waters, I cut myself
with a butter knife on bathroom tiles.
It's useless. They laugh at my antics. You were
at least half-convincing. There were windows,

god-awful in their openness or devious slits
in the blinds. Your father, that thespian,
carried his skull around as if poised to perform
Shakespearian monologue. Apostrophizing
into your beard, burying bones in the backyard
on high holidays, you knew how to keep

the ball bouncing. You dog, you tail-
wagging hungry fella, what wonders you harbored
in the nooks and crannies of your countenance.
And I'm sure we touch at certain points.
A dentist might marvel at the sharpness
of our canines. A psychoanalyst might unravel

the caution tape that mummifies
our mothers. But I am alive and I'm not going
to let Henry catfish me. My lyric "I"
is oil slick and merrily, merrily, confessing
supposed sins, a smiling Steamboat Willie,
with violent urges and whistling resourcefulness.

Steve Buscemi

I don't trust people with perfect teeth,
unblemished eyes, words
that ebb too pinkly
from pristine lips—I prefer

a face like a fender-bender,
the hunched henchman licking
salt from his greasy French
fried fingers. Blistered beak, bluntly
articulate, these ones appear

pure and cold as the porcelain
in a public toilet. On a plane
of convicts, slumped in vagrant
prayer—I see you there and I'm done

with the teetotaling, well-tailored,
upholstered in posters beside
leading ladies; give me the pricks,
the pissers, the ones who withhold
their tips from grey-eyed waitresses.
Give me the crooked paradise

of your mouth in a face that the world
seems to scaffold itself around.

On Symbiosis

I know how badly you want me
to be this poem. How, by candlelight

and tapestry, you prod your way
from solitude—a finger pressed

to the page like a stethoscope.
Lichen, oxpecker, composite

of life and the ontological
rot that's left in its wake,

here you are, dear reader:
Me, in a small green box

with a silver bow. I know
you've had enough of philosophy

and the mangy graybeards
that spout it. I know Bukowski's

a cretin and poor Mona Lisa
morphs into DaVinci each time

you trace her sidelong glance.
That's why I offer a truce,

a last inch of grace; I wager
my body as the male praying

mantis does, headfirst, swooning
towards transcendence or a jug

of gasoline ready to feed itself to fire.

Foramen Magnum

Chiari Malformation 1 is characterized by downward displacement by more than four millimeters, of the cerebellar tonsils beneath the foramen magnum into the cervical spinal canal.
   —The American Association of Neurological Surgeons

In rarified tongue, with mythic grandeur, we take this term,
meaning "great passage," dumping Dante's Italian

in a Tuscan trattoria, and reaching for those Latinate
heights towards which our bones have been growing.

Trendsetters and coelacanths, primates and argonauts,
give that gaping maw behind your mind a taste

of lemon sorbet, a pallet cleanse. A spoonful
of salvation to be carried across the Bering Strait

and the corpus callosum. But what happens when
breaks this plank? When thoughts get stopped

up like an autumn gutter? Look at this exquisite
still life: my skull, a dish, my brain, a fish fresh

out of flopping, dead-eyed, yet a subtle pulsing
from the optic nerve. Did I mention my condition?

The brain, braving all elements, breaches its stony
fortress going god knows where. What a headache,

to see this dumb snail trailing CSF down my back
and across every page of this manuscript. Call the Army

Corps of Engineers! Hide the Dead Sea Scrolls in
your fanny pack! We've got a real situation here,

this neural swamp a cottage industry of self-
pity and heroic parataxis. Uh-oh, there it goes

again, the brain, wearing a keffiyeh now to keep
the harsh sun out of its own folds. It thinks

it's getting somewhere and since thinking is all
it does, it must be. Hence, I am beholden to the god

of probability. What I mean is odds are every body's got
a fucking problem that some poor brain is expected

to fix, so I run a finger across the white sheen
of my thoughts and think: *nice, no moss.*

The Most Beautiful Suicide

As her last wish, Evelyn McHale didn't want anyone to see her body, but the photo of her death has lived on for decades as "the most beautiful suicide."
   —*Katie Serena*

It's easy to envy you, Evelyn, your death
simple as sinking into a sofa,

your repose collapsed carefully
on a limo's roof: left hand lifted

as if on the cusp of a thought,
ankles crossed, beads of glass

glint amidst your fallen frame.
I have, once or twice, considered

the stir of your hands on my
sinewy soul, so I can't blame him,

the photographer, for plucking you
from 1947 after an 86-floor drop.

Or, for that matter, Warhol who
reproduced your death in black-

and-white silkscreened squares.
How I wish you'd lift your head

so I could walk you north of Wall
Street and drift to a jazz club

where we'd sip Juleps and hold
hands under the table. Where

deep down I'd feel a twinge
of regret, a worry, that like all

these other men, I'm using you
to learn the word that's scrawled

beneath your brow.

Semi-Autobiography as SNL Cast Member

now black bags sag well below my eyes   i'm smiling sad
        and can't stop loosing my sadness into stern
winds and laughing faces   I spin down the oil slick lane
        a bowling ball in cahoots with the pins
did I mention   i'm pete davidson   or he is me
        shaolin pilgrim at the deli buying gatorade
baconeggncheese   I look diseased   shoplifted kingly
        in my yankee-fitted throne not quite
brando's kowalski but honing   an anemic attraction
        exuding BDE i've been fished
from a sea of mob wives newports GEDs   people regal
        as me a momma's boy with friends
who used to sling water balloon condoms   at city buses
        light cigarettes behind the handball court
like existential flares   and I'll never be colin jost or jerry seinfeld
        i swear and my arms look too scrawny in cardigans
my teeth chomp at the laugh track   my voice lacks that
        polished observational timbre that raised
pitch at the punchline   because i'm concerned with what's
        inside that gap between crowd
and stage   my jokes as serious as flaunting   kim k up and down
        this deadbeat borough buying her milk duds
at the atrium ferrying   her uptown for heavy petting
        pesto burrata wu-tang blasted through
monstrous speakers   as the pad fills with other   somber souls
        and i hover above myself thinking about our fathers
how they were ushered   from the least to best   known borough
        how they were fed so soberly into the moloch's mouth

In Preparation of Storms

This is it—

the black before. Over-priced
popcorn and previews
of caped crusaders crusading
in sequels to reboots.

This is the teapot
steeped in heat, the foreword
of westbound shadows
scripted on clouds. Shuttered

windows, sandbags, twine-
wrapped garbage cans. You
can hear Frank O'Hara insist,
you don't refuse to breathe do you?

And like Frank, you begged
to see the show, the forbidden
dark delights, obscenities
ascending to sighs. It's true,

you *have* been breathing.
Breathing and burning
a vanilla candle, as the eye
passes over the Bahamas and turns

toward the mainland. And why
wouldn't it want to watch us squirm
under its wrath, its Old Testament rage?
Sometimes a hurricane comes along.

It just happens. Or you make it happen,
something about high pressure
and low pressure sets it spinning
and all you can do is sit there

with your stubborn lungs,
their elastic rebellion.

II

Like Bartleby's

my rebellion buds from inside. It takes time. Trades in a cannibal
for a cubicle, inkblots, commas crashing like waves. It starts sea-horse-
sized in the chest and works its way into the abdomen's bleached coral
and troubled algae. It dies and is reborn. Thrumming deity, sour
sky. An empty matchbox and a castaway ashtray. Profane footnote
in the brackish machinations of a theoretical treatise
forever swimming toward the paper shredder. My rebellion's nothing,
it dies. Its jaw, slack as a ballot box. It was silent for years. Fired
from the veterinarian's office, the Dollar Tree, the Department
of Motor Vehicles. I fed it raw mackerel and Marx—any
savory thing I could lay my hands on. Quiet . . . lots of quiet. I
fed it Melville and lamplight. Spermaceti. It dies. It dies. But when
it's not dying, it lives recklessly: a pinup girl on an atom
bomb, a dead wall reverie, a preference to shoulder epiphany.

Resonance Imaging

Because I'm scared, because sound
winds itself around me
like a bat echolocating
my neuroanatomy—I run

through the long list
of World Capitals I know:
Bratislava, Kabul, Windhoek—
Yes, geography will save me.

Land, water, distances traversed
in the folds of the brain
they're scanning, coiled
like metal wires

clanging in the white
esophagus that's swallowed me.
The man behind the glass
knows the spin of my mind's

vinyl: drops a pin where
the stem slips from the skull.
I must escape his peristalsis.
I must walk the streets

of Algiers, fortify myself
in the Casbah quarter.
Why bother?—the sounds
stalk me: I hear the hammers,

I hear the house in the midst
of its cacophonous assembly.
I'm at a techno-rave
in Copenhagen: lights pulsing

recurrent beats, mapping
the body of a neon dream girl.
I float past a seascape:
salt, sails, and Baltic sighs.

I'm a sucker for sound—
I like to step inside it, or it likes
to step inside me and stretch
like an epoch, like a sunset,

pink sinking into an ocean.
I'm waiting here for my diagnosis.

Thelonius Monk

Give it to me straight. Give it to me ugly,
flopping, a half-dead fish, or forged
in the Devil's drunken hand. Let me know

how it is—Misfortune with no chaser,
no lemon, no salt, no rounded numbers,
mulled words. Give me your loose-lipped

sutra, your honeypot cudgel, your pleasant
discord, and crystallized twang. Enter the room
with atonal swag and admit that the cancer

crackles in me like a bonfire at twilight.
Tell me I'm sick. Knot the G clef
round my neck and slick back my hair

in mortal preparation. For weeks,
I've prayed for delicious recidivism, the night-
flower has tip-toed to my window,

heavy with whispers and a sibilance
that tickles the ear, slows the blood.
Dr. Monk, I'm all mixed up, shaken

by your thump, and love has been
squeezed from the mind's organ grinder.
Outlandish, enamored, drunk on your

wobbly odyssey, your lumbering elephant
grace, I place myself on your ivory altar
and wait to be hammered home.

Emerson Synecdoche

An earlobe climbed the lectern to tell us of our collective value.
Wake, he said, your sluggard intellect, lift those iron lids, cut
that transatlantic umbilical cord that siphons all sustenance back
to the motherland. Don't you feel it, dormant inside you, an American
consciousness? Isn't there a great man we can cobble from our piecemeal
anatomy? Eyebrows sat up in their seats, toenails shouted amen, a fist
liberated its fingers in an act of unabashed praise. So long had we suspected
there was something exceptional in this chunk of land we'd cultivated;
the eardrums heard it coming like the reverberations of a far-off steam engine.
In tophats and tailcoats, eyeballs sprouted up and down the coast, ready
to confront every refractory fact and translate the breaking sigh of each wave.
Take it all in, he said, the warblings of robins, the twisted syntax
of the Mississippi. Be the centipede, the milkweed, the bog and its
army of cattails, the tongue that laps up every last fragment.

At the Reception Desk

after billions of years of natural selection and a few
sleepless nights   my father drives me to the hospital
in a minivan   and brings me to a very kind receptionist
whom I tell to go fuck herself   hardly in the mood
to be somewhere   so sanitary   white walls   water cooler
a television   in each corner   through the front glass
I see parked cars and trees drooling sap   I remember
me there   five-legged and scared   scuttling between rows
of wood-framed chairs and the room's chiaroscuro

the me who tries to wipe away the shakes   the me
in morphological crisis   one moment   a waxwing
singing to myself   the next a moth caught in light
I crack into a jackal   blaze into Johnny Rotten
this hospital is a piss-stain and how dare they   pinned
to the lepidopterist's table   I pray   for a way out
no they say   I beg   I apologize to mom and dad
and God   *fuck you* I wail   amorphous   un-specied
as a tall man   in a white coat   with fingers
like spiders props open my mouth   and fills it with
polished rocks   ambered insects   little pills

Tabula Rasa

I am suffering, yes, from a chronic
colorlessness, a blasé

burden and stinks that grow
increasingly subtle. Every now

and then I stick wet fingers
in the socket, aiming

for a pleasurable jolt
but find only dumb current

thrumming in my mouth.
The moon is full of shit.

As are politicians, trumpeters,
anyone who manages to agitate

their soul into a brassy blare.
That's what I thought, before

the surgeon forgot his gloves
in my skull. Before I bugged

my kidneys and set tripwire
along the length of my liver. Now,

I'm a budding egotist. A walking,
talking magnifying glass with

its red eye fixed on the ants
that crawl up and down my spinal

canal. There are whispers, yellowish
hints of foul play pulsing

in my fingertips, thoughts
bubble over white blood cells,

suspicions percolate in lymph.
It is fatal. It is fetal. It is lead-

heavy, subversive and vicious, this wish
that the sickness exists. This hope

that the rope tongues its way
toward my neck.

5G Golden Shovel

after The Crying of Lot 49

Listen, this isn't about you or me or Nancy Pelosi,   I'm
          just saying do your own research. Read some Pynchon. Find the
     source,   the sun, that bright yellow eminence projector
set so lofty in the sky.   Of course, don't stare at
          it directly, but get a good sense of the
     people and places it stains with its light.   At night, the planetarium

forgoes its steel rotunda   and stretches all
          its constellations out on the actual sky: The
     Big Dipper, Orion's Belt, Ursa Minor. These doppelganger stars open closed
minds,   toxins are released, the little

things you've spent decades sweating shrink   as the universe
          expands another omnidirectional mile   and the known visible
     world leaves you   an unsatisfying voicemail. Again. You're in
a slump, but I've got just the
          drink to cure it—spiritually-infused, a citrusy circle

of conspiratorial liquids,   the fizzing of
          buzzwords. *Synergy*, yes,   and *vibrations* that
     suggest meaning and multiple levels of mass-marketed, stage
presence.   O Joy Reid   O Jesus   O Hannity,   is
          it enough that we stare at you   and think about the storm coming?

Will the algorithm cradle us to sleep   on a MyPillow?   Out, out!
            Even you Don Lemon! Bending language like copper wire, full of
      backward Beatles songs   and the affirmations of my
   Peloton trainer,   I hitch zip ties to my belt and mouth
            obscenities at the microphones lodged under the floorboards. All eyes

are on me now: the Postman,   the message carrier,   the sometimes
               prophet who weaves his words in the frequencies other
  souls are just starting to tune into. Here in the depths of the internet, orifices
  are what we are all so bent on becoming   and perhaps gods, also.

Ballad of Ted Williams

Ted Williams was decapitated by surgeons at the cryonics company where his body is suspended in liquid nitrogen, and several samples of his DNA are missing.
    –CBS News

Love is loaded with blood thinners
and packed in a body bag
with dry ice. Love is a charter jet
set for Scottsdale, Arizona.
A forged letter, a fake pact, to be
frozen and reunited in some
cryonically contained eventuality.
Godspeed Ted, I kid you not
your kids are keeping you
in a freezer, your severed head
atop a can of Bumble
Bee tuna. Splendid splinter,
love has a simple syntax
and words preserve, but
there is no crack-proof oracle
capable of holding
your wholeness. Love is
weird. Think Hannibal Lecter,
Bonnie and Clyde, think
hybristophilia—a guillotine kind
of getting off. Love is cruel
and cantankerous and crawling
like prehistoric insects on top
of an ice cream sundae.
I know you asked *to be cremated*
and sprinkled off the coast
of Florida where the water is
very deep, to slowly disintegrate
along with the memory
of your MVPs, but love
had to, of course, have its way
with your corpse, leave you transfixed
in a fridge by the desert.

Proposition

after Alfred Hitchcock

Something about the lure of the moon, the black-and-white
gloom of futon and Turner Classic movies, the sub-

suming chug of the train, pulls me to you, you
campy Raskolnikov, you backlit chatterbox, criss-

crossed legs and double scotch perched
on Promethean overreach. You muse, dear

Bruno, on the perfect murder, the ol' switcheroo,
the *you do me and I'll do you*, but how to

iron out the details? And does the plot matter as much
as the style? The deceitful lipstick, the voyeuristic

shut-in with his long lens longing for legs
that dance across the courtyard. Of course,

I've had the thought and followed it
up a winding staircase. I've rolled its smooth

weight between my fingers like a memento
mori marble, a lacquered pawn, admiring

the geometry of possibility. But what if
I get jittery? Or what if you double-cross me

as my inner ear condition sets the room spinning.
You leave me miles from the highway with no alibi

and a deviated septum? No, I don't trust your
fancy scripted tie clip, you devious francophile

with a father complex, you won't latch yourself
to me. Already I tread on your shadow, I gaze

into the alleyway's seductive dark and lust
for ways to end you. Oh, I won't hold back

for Hays codes or good taste; I'll creep
up to your peephole dressed in mother's best.

III

Void-Song

       I open Door after Door,   greening gold, wavy
      wheat stalks,   fields of them, lakes of them,
great rivers of Doors   straining upstream
like salmon, only to spawn   die   and birth
      new Doors. I will try all of them.
    They say in a fire to feel the knob first,
in the absence of heat   you may proceed.
I have never been so cautious:
      agape, agate, a grape-painted Door
      in a vine-green wall, I'll walk the gang-   plank
as the sea's heaves diminuendo, a silver Door
swallows me like a simoom—takes me
      to crestfallen hills of sand, takes me to a bar
      where a lizard king swirls his forked tongue
round a glass of merlot.   The Doors
will have nothing of this plain, New England
      existence, they like parchment and train tracks
      their hands want   to rearrange my vertebrae
and make a mansard roof of my skull.
I'm in danger   of letting go, of giving myself
      too completely.   I'm praying,
      Door after Door—O after O, beefy bold throats
take me away,   take me back
into your void-song, your whiplash   of womb,
      room, tomb.

Self-Portrait With an Open Skull

How cold this room, how baby blue
the sheets as I shiver myself to sleep.
I want to remember
what it was like: face-down:
scalpels, forceps, hands
intruding on a dream,
saws, clamps, breaking in
to the bone white theater.

A hole in me, how cold
the clamp, how taut the skin.
Sing, sing, bone saw, open
the passage my thoughts walk,
the frosted back alleys
of the brain, the seedy
side-streets with plastic bag
tumbleweeds, an anesthesia dream.

Godly cinematographer,
get that dolly shot
in the subway; show a rat
trekking a slice of pizza down
the tracks. This is where
one goes when the lights go
out, when sterile gloves tread
deep in the soul, this is where
the metronome of the mind is.

Then a waking, soft and slow
like walking in the corridor
between two lives. The lights dim.
A projector flickers and I see how
the bone saw let the light pour in—
sawdust, stardust, thought rust.
I see the surgeon's hands
and the paper moth
which he pulls from my skull.

Frances McDormand

Waddling into Fargo snow, 8-months plump, printing
a beeline that ceases at an overturned Chevy,

she hunches forward—*mornin' sickness*—but quick
as it comes it leaves, and she's left beside the deceased

craving a hamburger. Whether a boot, a bout, or about,
we know she'll find the murderer; we know she is tender

as a woodchipper and willing to post an advertisement
if that's what it takes to lessen the unremitting

migraine of her daughter's death. Don't be fooled
by how small she looks, crouched below a billboard,

planting tulips in a ceramic pot. She's capable of birth
and re-birth, of hardboiled and lovelorn, of knowing

the deer is a deer, but also her daughter. In reality,
she was an unmothered daughter adopted by a roaming

minister, a man who specialized in restoring congregations;
a connection we can't help but think of as she steps

onstage, straightens her back, and asserts, *I've got some
things to say*—setting diminutive Oscar down, she declares

herself an *inclusion rider*, and we see her: housewife
jackknife, on a motorbike, wrinkles flanking crow's feet,

ushanka shoved over her ears, as she tears past fuchsia
and wildflowers, gliding over a macadam of mourning.

Thoreau in Williamsburg

So I was never quite Crusoe. I had three roommates in my flat, two
who did PR for tech startups, one who brewed and bottled kombucha.
I lived off my own industry: selling hand-carved pipes on Etsy.
Dispensing orchids beneath the Brooklyn Bridge, twelve bucks a bloom. Three blocks
from the nearest bodega, I subsisted on strict rations of ramen
noodles whose salt stirred in me the burgeoning of an eastern philosophy.
There's something savory in asceticism. I kept a compost
of neem leaves and eggshells, the breaking down of organic matter
mirroring my own mental deliberations. I went there to get clear-
headed, to grow my beard and ride my Schwinn alongside the East River.
I wanted to unlatch myself from gold fetters and protest the taxing
8-hour days one lugs across the calendar. It is a coarse labor
with a forlorn budget, I'd think, departing the Wilco concert,
watching the old ways dissipate like smoke from my e-cig.

Scorsese Dreamsong

Drifting into taxicab transience,
a windshield's neon grimace, the love-

stripped streets of an indisposed city—I look for
what's graffitied in asphalt's marginalia:

dopplerized wail of an ambulance.
Prick of a campaign pin. De Niro,

in a wife-beater, aims his finger
at the mirror. No one trusts anyone, whip-pan

from mob boss to stoolie to starlet
flicking her cigarette into a heart-shaped

ashtray. And here's the hero, mohawked
in a studio apartment, scrawling fragments,

stocking cabinets with non-perishables
in preparation for the race war. A degenerate

bestiary flickers in a porno theater
as his date squirms in her seat—I'm latched

by these cells—between heaven and hell,
between close-up and wide shot of two

rival gangs collapsing on each other
with meat cleavers, fire pokers. Trying

to smuggle in grace like a shiv in a cake,
tired of the 9 to 5 hiding, I make

myself into a made man and grope
at the dark—thick black frames and untamed

eyebrows lead me to a limbo of smart-mouthed
excess; blood-stained, pin-striped, where I'm willing

to bash a skull in for the sake of subsistence
then pop an Adderall in Tammany Hall

and wait for the music to sour into propellers
and Gimme Shelter as momma's Sunday

sauce boils over on the stove.

Ode to R. Budd Dwyer

R. Budd Dwyer was a Pennsylvania State Treasurer who shot himself during a televised news conference.

To have two mouths, one for singing
and one for screaming bloody murder—

this is what the poet strives for, to speak
from the temples. Still, I promise no spectacle,

I will not make of me a puzzle, a humpty-
dumpty-put-back-the-pieces affair.

So I've spent some months groaning
in the dark, sinking into an ossuary

couch. So I sit on the stoop staring
at distressed brick homes. Grant me

these indulgences, this leftover thought
reheated in the microwave of the mind:

maybe I will not mend. Is it melodramatic
if some days I come home and hang

my skull and skin on the coat rack.
If some nights I dream up a man's

busted bust seeping lingonberry jam.
If I have a kind of morbid admiration

for R. Budd, his moxie and his manners,
how before he blew his brains out—

he stepped back and pleaded, *Please,
please, leave the room if this will…*

if this will affect you.

Yorick,

>you boring brute, you skin-
less, slack-jawed vase who won't
deign to be soiled by a brain. You
putz, propped at the end of my arm

>or commandeering my neck
with mindless musings, soliloquizing
to a crowd of molars, your dome now
The Globe and Shakespeare

>scampering through the afterlife
like a quill-legged crab. I pick you up
at a Spirit Halloween (K-Mart
Spectre) and can feel cheap plastic

>and dense meaning converging
on your cranium. Why wasn't
there once a whole gamboling mass
beneath your mandible?

>Remember when Mother, played
by a man finely powdered,
would beat the dust from her mat?
The world was still fresh

>in its cellophane wrapper
and Branagh, Zeffirelli, Welles
were tadpoles swimming in the
preface of that great tongue

>which came to lick literature to the big
screen. I can't swallow it, this jaw-
breaker, and it won't dissolve
the image of the man who bore me

>on his back a thousand times. As I suck
this memory, it occurs to me that I
look through your eyesockets, Yorick,
at the gravedigger with the gall

to unearth you. Has this fellow no feeling
of his business? Have these nights sifting
limbs of playwrights and plumbers
enameled his manners? It's lunacide

scraping leftover light from stark
naked faces. I can't even speak
to a skull without wondering
if it succumbed to cliché.

Decasia: The State of Decay

after Bill Morrison

who feeds me   this nightmare   fuel
this Rorschach of sun-   spots this mimesis
of macular degeneration   and Molotov
archaisms   black   bleeding into the
frame backed by an off-   tune orchestra
who said the dying   had to moan that Tut
in his tomb   embraced   a centuries-
long quiet when they scooped   his brains
through the nasal canal   iconic and
flammable   a nitrate montage   laps
the screen with its weatherbeaten tongue
a couple kissing   the threshold of non-
existence   their lips   kept distant
kids whirring   as the carousel warps
Yeatsian   and babes
just pulled from mothers'   loins have already
loosed mortal coils no wonder   i can
taste the   dustbin   no wonder i loan
my skin to Buffalo Bill   hoping
to warm his   tucked and unhinged shimmy
the universe sometimes seems to give
zero fucks   about our epistemologies and
chicken egg conundrums   our penchant
for filtering vocables   into dentures when time
eats   its way through   our molars

Bill Murray

If the legends are true, he turns up
in dive bars, strip clubs, aproned
and cradling two pots of joe in some

random deadbeat diner; his gravelly face
softened by the ripples of light
that protrude from such lowly places.

He ambles up to you from behind
and folds his hands over your eyes before
whispering, *no one will ever believe you.*

And maybe it's a game of improv, maybe
he's playing a fictionalized version of himself,
Bill *Ghostbustin' Ass* Murray, spontaneity

incarnate, mercurial deadpan remnant
of that one redundant day the 80s and 90s
now are. Maybe he roosts in the mind

like a half-remembered poem, ghostly
words grown gnarled on the tree trunk
of our consciousness. Or maybe he's a reminder

that no one ever believes who or what
they see. It's the feeling that counts,
the mythological assertion that we

are all accomplices to his holy cameo.

Another Dusky Sonnet

We open immediately: a delicious Dalí nightmare—black
and bleak, blinking eyes. A tempered smell of sulfur. Not a splotch of sun-
light. It's problematic, to say the least, a cliché meets another
cliché in an alleyway, bounds and gags it, drags it to a leather-
skinned sex dungeon—what happens there? I'd rather not say. Because the world
loves dream-logic, levitation, bones protruding from sand like dopey
marshmallows. A thought bristles inside of the skull—everyone you love will die
so you might as well squeeze them to dust. Like a podiatrist or a
soprano, you wrap your whole being around the tension, the full weight
of a body suffering gravity, and try to maneuver some
sweet grain of relief. It comes yodeling out, inappropriate, stark,
a treasure chest of muddy thrusts, a sestina of doubt, where at the end
of each line rests a clock that would rather not tick but melt, another
little death, cooing, rattling, sustaining itself on twilight's taut tongue

Digging My Own Grave

after Bernadette Mayer

When there's something to be said, I'm
capable of pulling my lower lip over my eyebrows, sorry
shoulders slump into a conscientious nihilism: *Nevermind
the deluge, the crude oil spill, the lyric "I"
stifled by the changing climate.* There was
an opportunity to make the killing spree just,
but my unconscious just wouldn't have it. Fiddlesticks! America is playing
with its pocketknife again, throwing around
complicated terms that make its gruesome business sound practical. I'm
not America all the time, but I am trying
to hide a blaring shame deep down in my psyche to
keep the specter of communism at bay; or, better yet, to find
a nice patch of grass in the cemetery of what
I pretend are my ideals. To be a poet I
kinda have to do this or at least guess
what virus LimeWire loosed in my mind while I
was daydreaming about Ted and Alice's foyer, and Dan Rather
jet skiing through his retirement. Obviously, comfort is not
something I take for granted, though I know
the splinter will come out if I move my tweezers more consciously.

Man on Bus #2

And all who know, know you
are not expendable. Sitting
beside a seven-figure salary, you

take things just as seriously, sulk
into a crossword as your foot thumps
the melody of the mundane.

You've bested, you've busted, you've
mouthed loose change like a metal
funnel: each arrival, each departure

accumulating in the credits of your
consciousness. Is it fair that the art
of your cross-legged khakis, the deft

yet zen-like strokes of your pencil
should stay peripheral to the plot?
That your late wife's pot roast

should elude even the simmerings
of a flashback? O you in who monotony
mourns, O you who never gets where

you're going, whose life juts adjacent
to beauties weeping away mascara,
as brooding directors pull strings

from accordion chairs. Brief candle,
poor player, let me swallow you
like a barbiturate, let me look into

your window like a lowly pedestrian
as the sermon of your sidelong glance frets
Tomorrow, and tomorrow, and tomorrow,

After Surgery, My Father Helps Me Bathe

Jobless, 26, a ghastly scab marching
        from the base of my skull down

my neck; beside me, my father kneels at the curtained
        threshold with a saucepan of warm

water. Steam obscures the boundaries between
        me and my past self, 6, smiling, slamming

the head of a red power ranger on faded
        ceramic tiles—oblivious, amphibious,

blanched in bathwater. My father sees me
        pruning memories and, politely, turns,

knowing well the subatomic gossip always
        whispering inside our bones. My father,

the policeman, who inhaled god-knows-what when
        the city really didn't sleep. When who he is now

stepped out from debris like a gray-tarnished twin.
        We are a kind of pentimento. Me and me

and him all living like stubborn
        brushstrokes in a gilded frame.

IV

The Rogue Patient

I haven't been happy since the hospital. One hall
and a flock of nurses, their faces, crow's feet
and white eyes over smokestack scrubs. Sorry
for them, I'd ask about their days, their kids,
their weekend plans. I sat by the window with one,
looking out into the parking lot at stray weeds
straining through cement. I asked if this was
a form of punishment or of help, she told me,
a little bit of both. At night we would line up for meds.
I thought about the movies, the rogue patient
who pretends to swallow, sweeping the mind medicine
under the tongue. I swallowed though. The brain
glazed over, the mind muddled grey. The nurse squinted
at my open mouth, pity billowed out in clouds.

Murphy's Law

30 rabies shots, my uncle got
when, after cornering a rat for fun,
and drunk, it lept and bit his bare chest.

Play stupid games, win stupid prizes, they
say—*what can happen, will*—Which is what
my dad was thinking when he passed the pub

so aptly named on the day they sawed
through my skull. This is the perversity
of the universe. You go outside

to catch your breath and butcher's knives wink
in every window. Miles' trumpet intones
"So What" while atom bombs dream of flouting

their dormancy. The night before surgery,
I lay on the plush hotel bed, staring
at a room service form. When I was

little, I was obsessed with opulence.
I wanted filet mignon, lobster
delivered to my imagined penthouse

as I watched cartoons: a toddler bobbing
along the steel girders of a nascent
skyscraper, pianos crashing down, turning

teeth into sonatas. I remember assuming
the hospital's food would be suspect.
Juice with plastic peel-off top, overly-

salted soup, but, I thought: that's only
if they don't slice into my temporal
lobe. If they don't accidentally

give me a lobotomy, or cut my
head clean off. Sometimes you have
to confront the world's malice like a mouse

who's been burned too many times by spring-loaded-cheese. Sometimes you're lucky to gag on pot pie while mom scrolls WebMD.

The Sunday Scaries

after Terry Gilliam

Yes, you can have it all within the space of a sonnet: love, escape,
the bulging trapeziuses of trapeze artists as they glitter
across the humbled above. Small and far as fear the workweek drones on
and a white suit steps from death carrying a briefcase of uppers and
downers and a tainted cigarette that will teach you how to shape
silence into strawberries. A more efficient form of desire,
the illusion need only be re-applied every hour. Sunscreen,
cooler, the calendar's upturned tongue, you pack for your mass-reproduced
vacation in the land of lilypad stilettos. Bats flicker in
and out of aviator shades as you lounge on an I-9 form, breathe
in the salty data of sea and sand. Cut-paper hand of God caught
picking its nose. A rabid horde of accountants stalks among the dunes.
I never had an hour glass's chance, you think, as the electric
billboard in the padded room expounds the sins of your credit rating.

Tilda Swinton

it is your body   I see powdered in
sleep   lithe and long and almost
saintly in its stillness   in this glass
box in Serpentine Gallery   an
exhibition   an object un-object-
ifiable   I follow the thin bridge
of your nose down to indifferent
lips and   a self-protective crook
of the arm above your mom-jeaned
hips   can we talk about Kevin

devil-spawn and beige awnings   life
with its steady whimpering of wonder
remember when you beamed down
androgynous   mystic   thieving glances
all Ziggy Stardust foreign lust and spooling loose
from the borders of yourself   remember
when they Woolfed you from noble-
man to wayward wench   as they tried
to fence a frame around your arthouse
body   your angelic ravishments most

surely shorn from sky   that's why
I'm struck by your skewed sense
the way you twist   your arms and contort
all grace from your neck   make me vivid
as dust tangled in spotlight   tune me
so a song gleams from the eyes that trespass
over my flesh teach me to collaborate
with lingering spirits   heron-like
white   in an unruly river

A Vindication

for Natalie

Ever since I met you I've been fighting the urge to apologize.
My fingers are, sometimes, stupid and I'm often overzealous, words
bursting like flares in uncertain skies, notes frenzying the felt innards
of pianos. The sandalwood scent, the sidelong glance of a foot lamp,
the careful work of your kidneys as they sort what's worth continuing
to circulate, all of these buzz in the background as a litany
of sorry synonyms slips the nozzle of my mouth: regret, contrite,
I beg for pardon, knowing the vernacular was meant to trap you.
The nightcap in Newport, the never-ending game of telephone. Love
notes I workshopped and sent soaring like paper airplanes across the classroom. Forgive me these deceits, these fussy phonemes I've fit to this old
form, none of which can contend with the cross-hatched glass of Seagram's gin
at golden hour, deep swigs, as you lament your ex's food allergies
and we dream about stuffing our faces with nightfall, peanuts, crawfish.

Love-Sloshed Cinema

I want you laced in celluloid—
the script torched, tossed—
This is not an act. It's love

as we learned it. Technicolor
big band: burly trombones—
I want you laced in tempestuous

trumpets, a slicked-back Sinatra
deepening night's hues.
This is not an act, it's love;

umbrella-less, rain-drenched,
Gene Kelly stomping down the wet set,
I want you. Laced in celluloid,

intoxicated, both of us, ruthlessly
ransacked, a deep-cut red dress,
not an act. I want love, Love,

sliding from a string quartet
as we melt into melodrama and gin.

Hook's Soliloquy

Aye, Smee; I was once young too. Suspiciously blue
were my mother's eyes. We took tea twice a day.
I hooked fingers in the dirt, feeling for earthworms,
centipedes, and those little insects that roll themselves

into marbles. I did not yet know the weight of a life
ebbing from a slit throat. It claws my heart, Smee,
how time comes ticking in its knobby reptilian suit.
Buoyant maelstrom, dagger in mouth, that insolent

youth, Pan, appeared. Dangled himself
like ambivalent bait. Twas he who gave that green
demon a taste of me. Twas he who cut me to
asymmetry. Smee, good breeding has done nothing

to nullify the ivy ropes that rule my mind. I hate
his band of sniveling boys and the inchoate
grief that shows on his lips each time he mouths *mother*.
Do you see it, Smee? That smidgeon of misery

in his frolic? That wisp of black behind the eyes?
It's his quietus that creeps inside my captain's quarters
late at night, stoops superciliously over my bed.
Plot the course, Smee. Tell the crew to quit their liar's

dice and mumblety-peg, tonight we sail toward
his light, we wave his shadow from our mast.

When You Come Around Everything Else Disappears

My eyes, of course. But also the sweet and sour sauce and the rest of
the appetizer, eaten out of sheer fright. Wax pooling round the wick.
I doubt you've your fill of calamari as the waiter grabs his tip
and tosses the doggy bag on my lap. Are my glasses on my hat?
Then ears, too, hightail it into twilight, flapping with lavish gusto
until, black-snagged, they spin in ceaseless circles like flies sprayed lethal
dosage of Raid. And aren't there Altoids somewhere in this satchel? Or
is it all talk, leather gabbing academic grift: love me, love me,
flutters off car keys and movie stubs as you slip through my buttery
and artificial fingers. *Quiet, bub, the trailers are starting*, you
mouth, as the projector spits our first date onto the screen. Where were we?
Oh right, just about night, we drop our inhibitions in a rocks glass
and pour sweet oratorios down the well. Time, too, disappears. Flip-
book calendar. Paris. The catacombs. Bones, bones, and us holding hands.

Sirens' Lexicon

for Natalie

Let's say we have a language. Let's say it's
mutually unintelligible, a mumbled armada

of terms anchored in the port of our mouths.
Let's say I'm out back in Adirondack

chair smashing nouns together, delighting in the spark
of your encouragement. Let's say my mother made me

an anxious boy. And I don't hate her for it. Let's say
I worry there are too many rings to count inside

each tree. Too many hypotheticals hovering
above trolleys. Dilemmas, fetishes

and photophores blazing in a leagues-deep dark
that knows not the timbre of your voice or the sun-

choke rooted in a friendly soil. Let's say you
recognize the enigma too. Let's say you spit

lyrics badder than Biggie's and flex
intersections of selves, corridors, and rooms that would

rival Virginia. Let's say we go to sleep. Walk
the gangplank into that same dream where

I'm welding, for the two of us, a periscope
that we can use, straw-like, to suck sights

into our submarine. It's not that
I want to sink deeper into shared solitude,

it's not the end or ore I look to excavate
from our twined lives, but a fore-

shadowing of feldspar, a lovecrank, a wordfire,
something real enough that, when we hear it,

they'll have to tie us both to the mast to keep
from tearing up the seas.

Chuang-Tzu Golden Shovel

The biggest pessimist on Instagram, you
post a roasted pig carcass and think
about its piglets. You
wince at the smell of apple cider vinegar. You do
and you don't. Erasure plagues you like a well
catching coppered worries, oh well—to
thrill at the bloody taste is worth it—hide
your nail clippings, prune the
Salieri-envy hanging from your forearms, little
black buds. They're no big deal these things:
Brutus, Judas, we're all chock full of betrayal, in
and out of love. Astronomer or botanist, the
only difference is what you choose to ignore. Big
planets or little seeds, these ones or those ones.

You are no oracle but
see a dark forest limned in light: slick what,
elastic who, purple when, cold if.
Listen to the heart's twang and croon, you
are the tone-deaf virtuoso. There were
blues songs and buttery biscuits to
slip into your esophagus, to hide
in your gut among the
flora. Now there is another world,
where the sky seasons you in
paprika, where brass chariots line the
streets—look inside your shirt pocket—that world.

Notes

The epigraphs for the book come from the following:
"The Cinematographic Principle and the Ideogram" by Sergei Eisenstein, published as an afterword to a pamphlet by N. Kaufman entitled *Japanese Cinema*.
"The Great Train Robbery" by A. Van Jordan from *The Cineaste*. Used by author permission.
Self-Portrait in a Convex Mirror by John Ashbery. Used with the permission of the John Ashbery Estate.

"Atmospheric Skull Sodomizing a Grand Piano" converses with Salvador Dalí's same-named painting (1934).
"In Defense of Voice-over" begins with the first words narrated in *Adaptation*. (2002), a film centered on a fictionalized version of its screenwriter, Charlie Kaufman. The poem's title responds to a screenwriting seminar that Kaufman attends out of creative desperation where script-guru Robert McKee (played by Brian Cox) asserts that voice-over is "flaccid, sloppy writing."
"Fast-Fish and Loose-Fish" takes its title from a favorite chapter in Herman Melville's *Moby Dick* (1851).
"Under the Water or Whistling" takes its title from the closing lines of John Berryman's "The Ball" in which he writes " . . . I suffer and move, my mind and my heart move / With all that move me, under the water / Or whistling, I am not a little boy."
"Foramen Magnum" concludes with an image inspired by Frank O'hara's "Song (Is it dirty)."
"The Most Beautiful Suicide" begins with an epigraph from Katie Serena's article in *all that's interesting* entitled "The Tragic Story Of Evelyn McHale, The Woman In The Infamous 'Most Beautiful Suicide'."
"Semi-Autobiography as SNL Cast Member" explores personal connections with Pete Davidson as we are both from Staten Island and sons of 9/11 first responders. The poem's ending reappropriates Ginsberg's Moloch ("Howl") to underscore the expendability of working-class first responders involved in the Ground Zero clean-up effort who were assured by Christine Todd Whitman, former head of the EPA, that the air in lower Manhattan "did not pose a public health hazard."
"In Preparation of Storms" takes the line "you don't refuse to breath do you" from Frank O'Hara's "Song (Is it dirty)."
"Like Bartleby's" is a poetic response to Herman Melville's classic short story "Bartleby, The Scrivener."

"Thelonious Monk" opens with lines that riff off of Thelonious Monk's album *Straight, No Chaser* (1967).

"Emerson Synecdoche" is inspired by Ralph Waldo Emerson's speech "The American Scholar." It also references his notion of the "transparent eyeball" which was later illustrated by Christopher Pearse Cranch.

"5G Golden Shovel" uses its golden shovel format to weave in a speech from Randolph Driblette, the delightfully unhinged theatre director in Thomas Pynchon's *The Crying of Lot 49* (1965).

"Ballad of Ted Williams" includes italicized language from Ted Williams's 1996 will.

"Frances McDormand" includes italicized language from Frances McDormand's 2018 Oscars acceptance speech for Best Actress in a Leading Role.

"Thoreau in Williamsburg" is inspired by "Economy," the first chapter of Henry David Thoreau's ever-resonant *Walden* (1854).

"Ode to R. Budd Dwyer" concludes with italicized language that R. Budd Dwyer spoke in the moments before his televised suicide.

"Yorick," includes part of the following quote from Act 5, Scene 1 of *Hamlet* : "Has this fellow no feeling of his business? He sings at grave-making."

"Decasia: The State of Decay" converses with William Morrison's same-named experimental film (2002).

"Digging My Own Grave" uses its golden shovel format to weave in language from Bernadette Mayer's brilliant maternal oddysey *Midwinter Day* (1982).

"Man on Bus #2" ends with language taken from the "Tomorrow, and tomorrow, and tomorrow" speech in Act 5, Scene 4 of *Macbeth*.

"Tilda Swinton" opens with a reference to a work of performance art entitled *The Maybe* (1995) in which the actress put herself on display within a large glass rectangle at the Serpentine Gallery in London."

"When You Come Around Everything Else Disappears" takes inspiration from indie pop band Of Montreal's quirky ballad "Everything Disappears When You Come Around" from the album *Cherry Peel*.

"Sirens' Lexicon" ends with a reimagining of Odysseus's solitary journey as a tandem adventure with one's lover.

"Chuang-Tzu Golden Shovel" uses its golden shovel format to weave in a quote from Taoist Philosopher Chuang-Tzu.

Acknowledgements

I would like to thank the editors of the following publications where these poems first appeared, sometimes in alternate versions:

Across The Margin: "In Preparation of Storms"
The American Journal of Poetry: "Ode to R. Budd Dwyer"
Bayou Magazine: "Atmospheric Skull Sodomizing a Grand Piano"
Bear Review: "When You Come Around Everything Else Disappears"
Beloit Poetry Journal: "Thelonius Monk" and "Sirens' Lexicon"
Bicoastal Review: "Tilda Swinton"
Cincinnati Review: "Proposition" and "A Vindication"
Colorado Review: "5G Golden Shovel" and "On Symbiosis"
The Common: "After Surgery, My Father Helps Me Bathe"
CutBank: "Fast-Fish and Loose-Fish"
decomP : "Void-Song"
Denver Quarterly: "Foramen Magnum"
The Florida Review's Aquifer: "Murphy's Law"
Frontier: "Another Dusky Sonnet"
Fugue: "Thoreau in Williamsburg"
Gulf Coast: "Semi-Autobiography as SNL Cast Member"
Leavings: "Rogue Patient"
The MacGuffin: "A Hypochondriac Walks into Fourteen Lines"
The Madison Review: "Like Bartleby's"
Midwest Quarterly: "Steve Buscemi" and "Bill Murray"
The Pinch: "Watching Jeopardy I Start to Feel Sad"
Prelude: "Hook's Soliloquy"
Radar Poetry: "Self-Portrait With an Open Skull"
Rhino: "The Sunday Scaries"
Salamander: "In Defense of Voice-over"
The Shore: "Scorsese Dreamsong"
Spillway: "At the Reception Desk"
The Summerset Review: "Resonance Imaging"
The Texas Review: "Decasia: The State of Decay"
Thrush: "Love-Sloshed Cinema"
Tipton Poetry Journal: "Ballad of Ted Williams"
Whiskey Island: "Chuang Tzu Golden Shovel"
Yalobusha: "Emerson Synecdoche"
"Murphy's Law" appears in the anthology *Best New Poets 2023*
"After Surgery, My Father Helps Me Bathe" was reprinted in *medmic*

My deepest gratitude to the friends, family, and mentors who were a wellspring of support and inspiration for this collection. Without your film recommendations, stories, and creative insights, my most significant publications would probably be on Letterboxd.

Thank you to David Kirby, Andrew Epstein, Christina Parker-Flynn, Virgil Suárez, James Kimbrell, Cate Marvin, Tyehimba Jess, Alessandra Lynch, Chris Forhan, David Shumate, and the many other amazing faculty members I've taken classes with at Florida State University, Butler University, and The College of Staten Island. You've each contributed to my poetics in invaluable ways, helping me to stretch language to its limits, find inspiration in unlikely places, and balance formal integrity with creative intuition. Your passion for the written word and commitment to knowledge and empathy is something that I will think about every time I get behind a lectern or pick up a pen.

To my former graduate school peers, especially Matt Zhao, Emilio Carrero, Brett Hanley, Lauren Howton, Dorsey Craft, Brett Cortelletti, Will Anderson, Isabella Tommasone, Max Lasky, Zuleyha Ozturk, John Leo, thank you for reading through draft after draft of these poems with open minds and hearts. Your imprint can be found on many of these pages.

A hearty thank you to the extraordinary Oliver de la Paz for choosing this collection as the winner of the Louise Bogan Award and to Kris Bigalk, Natasha Kane, Patrick Werle, and the rest of the Trio House Press staff for their editorial expertise and collaborative spirit. I could not have asked for a better and more understanding press to work with!

Mom and Dad, thank you for supporting me in something as silly as wanting to be a poet. Thank you for bringing me into this sometimes awful, sometimes beautiful world and for instilling me with the grit, ambition, and curiosity that it took to make this book.

To my brothers, James and Joey, your quick wit, intellect, and audacity often fueled my mind when I was wrangling these poems together. Thanks for always being there to converse on inscrutable indie films and for your worthy competition when we play along with Jeopardy contestants from the couch.

Natalie, maybe it's because I fell in love with both at the same time, but you and poetry are indistinguishable.

Thank you for being my literary comrade and for venturing out with me into strange syntax and far-flung diction. Because of your keen editorial eye and Piscean intuition, these poems hone their language more fully and boldly.

About the Author

Anthony Borruso is a poet, educator, and film enthusiast from Staten Island, New York. He holds a Ph.D. in Creative Writing from Florida State University where he served as a Poetry Editor for *Southeast Review*, co-hosted the Jerome Stern Reading series, and managed an incarcerated writers workshop at Gadsden correctional facility. His poetry merges confessional lyricism with examinations of pop culture artifacts and often meditates on the power of film in shaping one's identity. He is a 2023 Best New Poet and was selected as a finalist for *Beloit Poetry Journal*'s Adrienne Rich Award and Gigantic Sequins' Annual poetry contest. His poems have been published or are forthcoming in *Denver Quarterly*, *Beloit Poetry Journal*, *Pleiades*, *The Cincinnati Review*, *The Journal*, *Gulf Coast*, *Colorado Review*, and elsewhere. *Splice,* his debut full-length poetry collection, was a finalist for the Hollis Summer Poetry Prize and a semifinalist for the St.Lawrence Book Award and Minds on Fire Open Book Prize before being selected as the winner of the 2024 Louise Bogan Poetry Award by Oliver de la Paz. Anthony lives in Tampa, Florida, and is currently a Visiting Assistant Professor of Instruction at The University of South Florida.

About the Book

Splice was designed at Trio House Press through the collaboration of:

Natasha Kane, Primary Editor
Patrick Werle, Supporting Editor
Joel W. Coggins, Cover Design
Hadley Hendrix, Interior Design

The text is set in Adobe Caslon Pro.

About the Press

Trio House Press is an independent nonprofit press based in Minneapolis, Minnesota. We publish poetry and prose that moves, inspires, and encourages connection, empathy, and understanding, with a special emphasis on underrepresented voices and topics. To find out more about Trio House Press, please visit our website at http://www.triohousepress.org